CHRISTENDOM
IN DUBLIN

G. K. Chesterton

CHRISTENDOM IN DUBLIN

Personal impressions of the 31st Eucharistic Congress
Dublin 1932

With a preface by Peter Costello

THE IRISH CATHOLIC
Dublin 2012

The Irish Catholic
St Mary's, Bloomfield Avenue, Donnybrook, Dublin 4
www.irishcatholic.ie

First published by Sheed & Ward, London, November 1932;
reprinted November 1932, December 1932.
First published in the United States of America
by Sheed & Ward, New York, 1933.
This new edition published by The Irish Catholic June 2012

Typographical arrangement © The Irish Catholic 2012
Preface & notes © Peter Costello 2012
ISBN 978-0-9572743-0-3

Typesetting and design by Brian Murphy
Printed in Ireland by the Johnswood Press

This edition is published by
The Irish Catholic
on the occasion of the
50th Eucharistic Congress in Dublin
June 2012

PREFACE

By Peter Costello

The Eucharistic Congress held in Dublin in the summer of 1932 was one of the most important public events in the short history of the Irish Free State, then a mere decade old. It outshone the celebrations a few years before to mark the centenary of the passing of the Catholic Relief Act of 1829, an event known in Ireland as Catholic Emancipation. The official celebrations of that event had been on a grand scale, but were merely a prelude to the far greater pomp of the Eucharistic Congress, for which the fledgling State, still recovering both from a devastating civil war and from the effects of the economic down turn at the end of at the end of 1929, pulled out all the stops. The result was a truly memorable event.

The Congress brought G. K. Chesterton to Dublin. He stayed

as the guest of the King's representative in Ireland, the governor-general James McNeill, in what had been the Vice-Regal Lodge in the Phoenix Park. He was to write about the event for an English Catholic newspaper, as well as an Irish journal; and this little book is the final form of those articles, recording his personal impressions of the event in Dublin in June 21-26, 1932. By way of a preface to this special reprint something ought to be said about Chesterton himself and his relations with Ireland, as well about the event itself.

Gilbert Keith Chesterton, born in 1874, was then at the height of his fame as a writer and a public personality. He was most famous perhaps for his Father Brown mystery stories, featuring a seemingly disorganised, but deeply insightful, Catholic priest as his detective. Oddly enough, the very first Father Brown story, "The Blue Cross" (published in *The Storyteller* magazine in September 1910) was set at the time of the 22nd Eucharist Congress held in London, which provides the immediate impetus to the opening of the tale.

That congress had been held in Westminster from September 9 to 12, 1908. It had not passed without controversy: Herbert Asquith, the British Prime Minster of the day, under pressure from Protestant evangelicals, banned the public procession of the Blessed Sacrament through the streets around the Cathedral which was to have been the climax to the Congress. By contrast, in 1907, for the previous congress at Mainz in Lorraine, the German government had suspended the 1870 laws which precluded the holding of public religious parades in that country.

The Dublin Eucharistic Congress provided an almost complete contrast to that held in London. The new Irish Free State was only too happy to lend all its resources to the Catholic Church to achieve an internationally recognised success. It would prove to be a model of organisation, belying those critics abroad and in the North of Ireland, who thought that the Free State would soon display what they believed was its inherent incompetence.

Fr Brown himself was freely modelled on Chesterton's old friend an Irish parish priest in England named Fr John O'Connor. This is an early aspect of Chesterton's involvement with things Irish. He had written about the Celtic revival back in the 1890s, and was friendly with many Irish writers and public figures. In the years leading up to the Great War, when Home Rule was under vigorous debate, he wrote about Ireland from the Liberal point of view.

After the war he visited the country in 1919, setting down his reactions to the still developing situation in his *Irish Impressions* (London: Collins, 1919). He was in Ireland again for the first of the revived Tailteann Games ("the Celtic Olympics") held in Dublin in August 1924. This had a strong cultural aspect to it, with awards for poets and writers, and the fêting of honoured guests such as Chesterton, Compton Mackenzie and Sir Edward Lutyens.

During this visit he also attended a reception in his honour held at the recently established Central Catholic Library (then at 18 Hawkins Street). This was attended by the President of the Executive Council and Mrs William Cosgrave, Sir John and Lady Glynn, Colonel Maurice Moore (the Nationalist brother of novelist George Moore), General Richard Mulcahy and his wife, poet Padraic Colum and his wife Mary Colum the critic, and many other distinguished Catholics with literary interests.

In 1929 Chesterton, along with his friend and co-controversialist, Hilaire Belloc was awarded an Honorary Degree by the National University of Ireland — part of its celebration of the centenary of Catholic Emancipation — as distinguished Catholic writers of the day.

The creation of Father Brown in 1910, as well as such early books as *Orthodoxy*, has left many people with the impression that Chesterton was even then a Catholic. This is not the case. He was born an Anglican. Many of his still widely read titles from those early days, such as *Orthodoxy* (1908) are the works of an Anglican apologist and not a Catholic. He did not in fact convert to Catholicism until 1922, a full two years after his wife.

But once he had, so to speak, "gone over to Rome", Chesterton became, like many others converts, an energetic champion of the Church. And it was in this role that he came to Ireland in the summer of 1932 to attend the Eucharistic Congress.

These congresses had begun at Lille in France back in June 1881. Political circumstances under the Third Republic were not friendly to the Catholic Church. The idea behind the Eucharistic Congress was to provide some counterweight to official anticlericalism. The early congresses, following the original inspiration of the moment, were held in francophone countries. But in 1893 the Eucharistic Congress became truly international when the 8th was held in Jerusalem, then still under Ottoman rule. Eventually other locations in North America were visited. Finally, for the 31st Congress, the city of Dublin was selected.

At that time the government of William Cosgrave's Cumann na nGaedheal party was in power. But by the time the time the delegates arrived and the Congress got under way, the government had changed, and Éamon de Valera's Fianna Fáil party, which won the election in March 1932, was now in power with the support of the Labour Party. It was said in Dublin that the top hats of the Cosgrave years had given away to the soft hats of

Fianna Fáil, and indeed there was a slightly ostentatious wearing of lounge suits on the part of the new minsters rather than morning dress, that surprised some European visitors.

The head of state, however, was still George V, represented in Ireland by the governor-general, James McNeill; and McNeill in due course felt himself seriously snubbed by the new government, over anxious to assert its independence of the King's representative. However, these political and diplomatic manoeuvres are essentially a minor matter, of merely transitory local interest, in the total impact of the Congress.

It would be true to say that the Irish people surprised themselves by what took place. The organisation was excellent even down to the relaying around the world of the broadcasts of these events by the relatively new Irish radio service. The little shrines and the gay decorations that sprang up, not just in the back streets of Dublin, but all around the country, delighted visitors as evidence of the people's deep faith. There were still visible signs of raw poverty, but these rarely made their way into the official records, an exception being a rare illustrated brochure published by a Dutch sodality group.

The events of the Congress as seen by a friendly eye and creative pen are what Chesterton provides us with in this book; and the reader will be able to appreciate his impressions for themselves. The first four chapters were published in a London newspaper during and after the event; the last chapter in the Irish Jesuit quarterly *Studies* in November 1932, just before the publication of the book in London and New York. In the appendix to this edition an early essay on the Irish literary revival and national identity is reprinted; this did not form part of the original book.

To many the success of the Eucharistic Congress seemed to reinforce the link between Catholicism and Irish nationality. But this may well be an illusion. The Congress represents the summit of developments that had been going on to elevate the Church into a special position in Ireland – one which would be explicitly recognised by the new Constitution which de Valera would introduced in 1937 – that had been going on since the Synod of Thurles in 1850.

But from 1932 onwards there began a slow whittling away of this position, a slow decline in prestige. Ireland could not maintain a Catholic state for a Catholic people, to reprise the famous phrase about Northern Ireland. Elsewhere, in Germany, Austria, the United States, Great Britain, and even in Italy itself (where the Lateran Treaty of 1929 had established the Vatican State), the Catholic church had been forced to create new relations with the modern state. It was inevitable that in Ireland too the Church would have to reach an accommodation with the forces of the secular world.

This was a short time in coming. The events of the Mother and Child scheme in 1952 demonstrated not strength on the part of the Church, but weakness – if the power were real there would have been no thought of a challenger by the Minister of Health, Noel Brown. Indeed the whole church administrative system of Archbishop McQuaid at that time suggests not so much confidence so much as a deep grained fear. From there to the Second Vatican Council was but another short step, and from those hectic days of renewal continuous changes led to the more controversial developments of today.

Less debatable is Chesterton's career after 1932. He was then writing a series of lively Catholic biographies and essays. He died in June 1936. After that there was a dip in his reputation, but his fame as a writer lasted through to the end of 1960s. Then perhaps, what with the changes in literary and religious culture after Vatican II, he suffered an eclipse.

However, in more recent years, especially in North America, interest in Chesterton has increased. He still retains far more readers I suspect than many of his Catholic contemporaries, such as Hilaire Belloc, Maurice Baring, R. H. Benson, or D. B. Wyndham Lewis do. His literary and apologetic books are increasingly popular today, and for a writer born in 1870s that is an achievement. He has become in his own way a classic writer.

This little book is his most significant work on Irish affairs. But Ireland will long recall him as an Englishman who was always and everywhere the friend of the finest aspects of Irish culture, Irish literature and art, and of the Irish soul.

June 2012

CHRISTENDOM IN DUBLIN

CONTENTS

Preface by Peter Costello

I

THE FLUTTER OF THE FLAGS

DUBLIN is full of flags; and London is full of stories about flags. And it will be very difficult to explain to die-hard Londoners that Dublin, which is full of flags, is not thinking about flags at all.[1]

It is a perfectly natural misunderstanding; and indeed the misunderstanding is not all on one side. It has been said that patriotism is the religion of the English; and certainly the English greatness and glory have grown up in an age after the mediaeval development had given great importance to flags. Englishmen understand men rallying round a flag. They will not understand so easily that these Irishmen, during these seven days, were not rallying round any flag. It was the flags that did the rallying; they were rallying round something else; and it did not matter much, as a rule, what dogs they were. When it was reported that somebody had pulled down the Union Jack, most of the Irish I met thought it a very silly thing to do; some of them insisted that the flag should be replaced; some probably Celt equally annoyed at its being pulled down and at its being put up. All that

[1] The allusion is to the London Economic Conference held at this same time in South Kensington which was attended by representatives of 65 nations to discuss how to resolve the then serious world economic Depression. Ed. note.

really happened was that one silly little nobody and busybody removed it from one hotel; not from its official place, where it was officially displayed. But when the modern English hear of it, they are hardly to blame if they say things that are not so much on the wrong side as entirely on the wrong scale. The picture in their minds is all wrong. They think vaguely of Dublin Castle as a great tower above Dublin, with a Union Jack flying on it, and a horde of ferocious Fenians, with long upper lips, concentrating on the one purpose of pulling it down. Nothing of that sort happened; or could possibly have happened. A good many poor people in Dublin might be annoyed by seeing the Union Jack. But they would be annoyed because they were not thinking about it, not because they were. If a singer like John McCormack were passionately pouring out his favourite song, he might be annoyed at being suddenly prodded with a parasol by a Calvinistic great-aunt from Belfast, supposing him to possess such a relative. But he would be annoyed because he was not thinking about his great-aunt; not because all his thoughts were fixed day and night upon her. Nor would those annoyed at the interruption be altogether unreasonable in regarding it as an inter-ruption.

As a very sensible Irishman said in a letter to a Dublin paper: "The Union Jack is not the national flag of England." The national flag of England is the Cross of St. George, and that, oddly enough, was splashed from one end of Dublin to the other; it was mostly displayed on shield-shaped banners, and may have been regarded by many as merely religious; but it was the authentic St. George's Cross; gules on a field argent, with the four arms of the cross meeting the edges of the flag. The Union Jack, as its name implies, is the flag of the Union. Many might not unreasonably ask: Why should either England or Ireland want to wave the Union Jack in Dublin, when both England and Ireland had agreed to abolish the Union? It must also be remembered that, to the Dublin populace, the Union Jack is not so much the popular flag of the English people; it is the party flag of one Irish party; the old Orange party of Ascendancy. There were any number of reasons for people not liking the look of it; but there were only two instances of anybody wanting to interfere with it: one of which was instantly frustrated and reversed by the Irish authorities, who put the flag back again.

But the fundamental falsity in the discussion lies in the very meaning of the word "flag". The people were not hoisting any flag or hauling down any flag. The people were waving rags, and ribbons, and scraps of silk, and bits of paper, and anything they could lay their hands on, in frenzied salute to something that does not happen to be a flag; because it is about a thousand years older than the first flag that ever was made, somewhere in the Dark Ages; something that rose first to confront the old Roman ensign, which was only a pole, with an emblem on top of it.

The overwhelming majority of the flags, even in the formal official decorations, were simply gaily coloured pennons of no significance at all. The three significant flags commonly used were the Papal flag, the flag of the Congress, which was blue with a cross of gold, and the green, white and orange which make the tricolour of the Irish Free State. There were no national flags, or hardly any, in the ordinary sense. I never saw the French flag or the German flag or the Italian or Russian or Japanese flags, as one sees them on an English flag day. I saw the American flag once; I think over the American Consulate.

But the presence or the absence of such things were alike of the nature of accidents; because the substance of the whole was, so to speak, of a different stuff. The type of enthusiasm was not of that military sort that salutes a particular flag. It was not so much flags as flag-waving; not formality so much as frenzy; it was as if the flags were flames and all the houses had caught fire.

Nobody wanted anything at all except to cover the walls somehow with colour and movement. It was not even the wearing of the green; it was more like painting the town red.

But before I leave the last point of decoration, or at least of political decoration, may I make a suggestion? If this question is ever again discussed, let us hope in a friendly fashion and without further rupture, I would myself move a very simple amendment. If somebody does feel strongly the need of displaying the united colours of the old British kings, it would be a thousand times better in every way to fly the Royal Standard.[2]

It would be more logical and even more legal and constitutional; since admittedly, from the most British standpoint, the King is now the link between the two nations. It would also have the advantage, to which I cannot be blind till I am afflicted with blindness, that the Royal Standard is an exceedingly beautiful flag; and the Union Jack (I am torn by the duty of bearing testimony to aesthetic truth) is an exceedingly ugly flag. The reason has nothing to do with our political history; it is merely one of the facts of artistic history. The quarterings and colours of the Royal Standard were designed in a good artistic period; the period of real heraldry. There is a definite decorative quality in the golden leopards of Normandy or the red lion ramping among the red lilies. The Union Jack was designed in a bad artistic period; when heraldry had long decayed, and people could only combine three flags by turning them into a tangle of ugly stripes like a quilt. Some of us may think it was a bad period in other ways; some of us may have dark and bitter convictions that the

---

[2] The Irish Free State was still at this time a dominion of King George; but the flying of the Union flag in the 26 counties was often a contentious issue. Flying the Royal Standard would have been seen as just as provocative by Irish nationalists. Ed. note.

Union was as bad as the Union Jack. But these opinions have nothing to do with this particular opinion. It is simply a question of taking our flags from a period when people knew how to make flags, and not from a period when men had forgotten how to make them. Anybody can see the difference who will look at the three crosses of the Union Jack when they are separated and not confused. One of the most beautiful flags in the world was the old popular Scottish flag, which was called the Blue Blanket; the silver saltire on the azure ground; but the corresponding red cross of St. George is equally harmonious and conspicuous. And they could easily shine side by side, in times of peace and unity, as clearly as they must have shone against each other at Flodden or Bannockburn. But I do not draw here any political moral from the fact that they are much more harmonious when they are not united. I only say, in the name of anybody who has eyes in his head, that it certainly is a fact.

But my purpose in putting first this note about the fluttering of the flags is to soothe all those who made such a flutter about them, by assuring them that there was quite another spirit of gaiety about their fluttering. It is that strange spirit, and especially that strange gaiety (for it is strange to the great mass of the modern world) that is really worthy to rouse a certain reasonable curiosity; even in a man of the world. There is something here that is at least as well worth understanding as Bolshevism or Fascism or the Nazi movement. And I shall try to make it a little intelligible, even to those who hate it as heartily as I hate Big Business or Bolshevism. In other words, it was about something; and it was not about pulling down the Union Jack. It cannot be understood by the ordinary controversies about public questions; it was not even to be found most fully and vividly in the most public places. It was something in the populace that was not only not political, but not even in the ordinary sense national. At least, it was only national in the sense that it has happened to survive most strongly in a particular nation. It has a psychological interest for people to whom it has no philosophical appeal; and the great danger in the international relations is still to be found, not so much in people not liking it, as in people not knowing it is there.

As to what it is – that is perhaps best represented in the most extraordinary of all the experiences of a traveller and a sightseer in that town at that time. I mean the quite indescribable and unique character of the popular decoration, of what may be called the purely domestic decoration, in the very poorest quarters of the city. It is here that we find the presence of something almost without parallel on earth; and certainly quite without parallel in England. We may call it comic; we may call it creative;

we may call it crazy or impudent; we may call it an outburst of barbaric fancy and imagery; we may call it all sorts of things, according to our particular taste of culture. But it is something in the most emphatic sense worth seeing; as the people on another planet would be worth seeing.

When I first landed at the harbour of Dublin, there merely flashed through my mind, in the flash of the shining water and the ship, the line of the old passionate patriotic song: "The French are in the Bay"; and I thought with many mingled feelings that now at last the French were in the Bay with the Germans and the Italians and many more; met in a truly international mission, of which the men who sang that angry song had hardly dreamed. Then I was driven up the long roads to the city, and through the city; and these were all decorated in a dignified and even formal fashion, with great festoons of green garland going from lamp to lamp, and blazoned shields and a whole civic and centralised scheme of decoration. It was a very good scheme of decoration; but even here it is essential to emphasise the fact that it was not in the remotest fashion connected with faction or even opinion. There was not one touch or trace of politics, let alone party politics. Every emblem was of a sort unfamiliar today to most of the civic rites of civilisation. They were all the symbols we are accustomed to see in picture galleries; or, if we have any such eccentric curiosity, in churches. There were the Lamb and the Dove and various animals fabulous or real, who were symbols of mediaeval mysteries. I saw in one place the Fish; the most ancient of all Christian symbols; that awful fossil from the first substratum of death; of the days when a Christian must be as dumb as a fish lest he be destroyed like a snake. No; all that long and elaborate line of pageantry was not political; but it was official. The extraordinary fact about it was something that was quite unofficial.

The extraordinary thing was this. I have driven through many such arcades and triumphal arches in many such festive cities. And of nearly all of them it was true to say that any man who strayed from those festive highways would find the festivity fading away. He would find more or fewer flags in this or that side-street; he would not even expect to find so many as there were in the main street. In this one festivity all that common sense was reversed. It was truly like that celestial topsy-turvy-dom in which the first shall be last. Instead of the main stream of colour flowing down the main streets of commerce, and over-flowing into the crooked and neglected slums, it was exactly the other way; it was the slums that were the springs. There were the furnaces of colour; there were the fountains of light; it was as if whatever hidden thing shone here and there in those passionate transparencies was shining in the darkest place; as if the dark heart of the town pumped forth that purple blood, ending in a mere trickle along the highway. I know no other way of describing it; for I have never seen anything like it in my life.

In that strange town, the poorer were the streets, the richer were the street decorations. They were decorations of a queer kind, as may well be imagined; and yet the decorations were really and truly decorative. They had that triumphant harmony that comes from the complexity of crude colours; for colours always harmonise as long as there are enough of them. That is the secret of much Oriental art; and in that sense these mean streets glowed and glared like Oriental bazaars. But there was something in them that is freshness; or the spirit of something that is born again. I felt in a nameless fashion that I myself was born again; and was passing through a sort of supernatural toyshop. All that we feel in infancy about coloured lanterns lit suddenly from within, or peep-shows revealing vividly coloured figures and landscapes, or magic flowers that are made to open by a conjuring trick – all that secret dawn of infancy inhabited those blind alleys and black corners of Dublin. As in a transformation scene, walls might have grown transparent; there were changes in substance and in light.

Men who could not paint had painted pictures on their walls; and somehow painted them well. Men who could hardly write had written up inscriptions; and somehow they were dogmas as well as jokes. Somebody wrote, "Long Live St. Patrick"; as hoping that he might recover from his recent indisposition. Somebody wrote, "God Bless Christ the King"; and I knew I was staring at one of the staggering paradoxes of Christianity.

I went through all this glow and glory of poverty quite bewildered; only feeling that I was passing an endless series of sacred Punch-and-Judy shows or angelic toy theatres. I will not attempt to describe that ragged splendour any more fully at the moment. There were other aspects of it, of which more might be written in another connection. I think the main mark of it was moral courage. Perhaps I ought rather to say spiritual courage. I fear the poor of many another more prosperous town would have had what is called an inferiority-complex in the matter. One nameless impecunious person, in a slum, heard that the Legate was coming and laid down a red carpet on his doorstep.

Somehow I fear that few people in Hoxton[3] would have had the moral courage to make such a preparation. But, for the moment, there is only one thing to be said about my feelings, when I had passed through all these rags and tatters and patches of flaming and almost raging colour. I had forgotten all about flags.

---

[3] Hoxton is a district of London, just north of the City, between Finsbury and Bethnal Green, once infamous for its poverty and lawlessness; towards the end of the 19th century it was called "a sink of iniquity with hardly a parallel in England", a slum far worse than anything in Dublin. Ed. note.

And yet, at the last, there lingers in my mind the memory of a single flag: an example that may be called an exception. Sundered by leagues of distance, in a complete contrast of silence, seemingly remote in every way from the thronged and flag-waving city, there was something else that had a moral of its own. Of all the things I saw, it gave, perhaps, the greatest shock of novelty or incongruity to an Englishman. And yet it was something that could have been seen all over Ireland. For it was Ireland and not Dublin that celebrated the Dublin Congress. Yet, as I say, the particular form it took was, even to a sympathetic Englishman, queerly and quietly startling. Yet it was only the experience of driving away into the Wicklow Hills, miles and miles out of sight and sound of the city, in a rolling country of down and woodland, of "hollow lands and hilly lands," like those in which the poet made his mysterious pilgrimage. Huts and homesteads seemed to be few and far between, and to be growing fewer; and it was in such a lonely place that a man might find a last lonely homestead, seemingly a hundred miles from anywhere; and flying the Papal Flag.

As if it were a castle. Almost as if it were an enchanted castle. There was something unearthly, as of a place on which the ends of the earth were come, about that low neglected roof and that remote blazonry of Rome. An Englishman is accustomed to associating Ireland with little local shrines, till he has almost come to feel as if the saints were local; as if St. Peter had grown as Irish as St. Patrick. But to find tucked away, in a corner of the county, that is in a corner of the country, that is in an extreme corner of the continent, that standard which is called imperial, which is certainly international – that was like the linking of the most intimate and the most incredible distant things. It was truly the place where extremes meet. A priest may be found anywhere, from Ludgate Hill to Lapland, and he will generally be a good Englishman or a good Eskimo. But this was like finding a Papal Guard, with helmet and halberd, standing outside a thatched cottage in Westmoreland. And yet, I suppose, the sharp instantaneous incongruity only means that an Englishman is more insular than an Irishman.

Indeed I know well that what I, as an Englishman, only felt as incongruous, many other Englishmen feel as insolent. It is part of the picturesqueness of the thing that the Papal Flag is not a devotional or delicate thing; it is a tower of crowns and a parade of keys. Above all, its white and yellow are meant for silver and gold; and that exclusive pride in precious metals might well seem to be as defiant of humility as of heraldry. I have always said that I understand that disapproval; only I understand other things as well. That gold-and-silver standard of the triple crown really is in one sense an imperial flag; almost an imperious flag. Yet it was so homely to this wayside home that they hung it out like so much washing. That is where an Englishman gets a glimpse of another history and a new slant or angle upon Europe. It is the same with the apparent arrogance or opulence of the symbol of silver-and-gold. It will be generally found that, if there is really anything to be said against Catholic priests, it has been said by Catholic saints. The best anti-clerical jokes were made by clerics. And there is a story I have seen told of St. Dominic, though it is probably a tradition that might be told of anybody; that when he was shown the Byzantine glories of the old Vatican, with its gold and mosaic and metalwork, the Pope half humorously recalled the story of St. Peter granting a miracle because he had no money to give to a beggar. "You see," said the Pope, laughing, "Peter can now no longer say, 'Silver and gold have I none.'" "No," said the Friar, "and neither can he now say, 'Rise and walk.'"

I continued to stare, I know not why, at that little lonely house with that large and lordly flag. In the first flash of the fantastic, it had seemed as if the house could have been wrapped up in the flag; but as I looked more closely, I saw the house was larger than I thought, being low and rambling, with outhouses; being the small farmhouse of what seemed to be a very solid and prosperous farm; I saw the people moving to and fro among the barns, going about their duties as the sun went down. And I began to remember the other side of the argument and the end of the story. These men, now tilling their own soil, had once been hunted in it as modern laws would hardly suffer us to hunt wild beasts. The Irishry had hardly been treated like a race, but rather like a rash; like a disease that had broken out upon the soil and must be suppressed. They were hardly men, they only existed in the plural like measles. Fine poets and fastidious gentlemen, sent over from England, could only screw up their noses and suggest that some insecticide should remove the very smell of such sub-human humanity. It became not only sub-human, but subterranean; its creed was driven underground; its culture and language were assumed to have already died out, like the Aborigines of Tasmania[4]. And then, as if in a dream, it seemed that the scene altered and all the world was changed; and old powers began to play new parts. .. "The poor should as far as possible become owners." . . . The wiser statesmen of the later nineteenth century begin to hear older and more universal theories of the State, more generous than a cheap Radicalism or a tribal Toryism; property as a natural right of men and not a legal privilege of lucky men; economics as the servant of ethics; the servant of the servant of God. I looked again at the great gold-and-silver

[4] Tasmania is an island the size of Ireland to the south of Australia, with a similar temperate climate; the native people of which were driven into extinction by the white settlers, many of them Irish by 1876 – though one putative last survivor was later recognised and supported by the government down to her death in 1905. Ed. note.

banner and suddenly forgot all the nonsense about national and political conquest; and the idiocy that imagines the Pope as landing on our shores with a pistol in each hand. I knew there was another Empire that has never declined nor fallen; and there rolled through the heavens of pure thought the thunder of the great Encyclicals, and the mind of the new Europe in which the new nations find that the Faith can make them free. The great flag began to flap and crackle in the freshening evening wind; and those who had been toiling on the little farm, those whose fathers had been hunted like vermin, those whose religion should have been burnt out like witchcraft, came back slowly through the twilight; walking like lords on their own land. . . . Whatever St. Dominic may have said in the irritation of the moment, I am not so sure that St. Peter has lost the power to say, "Rise and walk."

II

THE ENDS OF THE EARTH

THERE is nothing that I enjoy so much, in the ordinary way, as taking a ticket and a train and a boat and going to Dublin. There is much in Dublin of what has always been said about Paris. It is an indescribable liveliness and lucidity; as if it were morally what it is certainly not materially; the *ville lumiere*; the legendary place in the sun. But there is something else to understand, about the extraordinary experience of the thing called a Eucharistic Congress. It was not merely this; perhaps it was not mainly this. It was something altogether different and astonishing; though it doubtless included this. I did not merely take a ticket for Holyhead, or a boat for the port of Dublin.

I did truly take a ticket for Christendom. I took a train and a boat that brought me to the ancient, and perhaps long-undiscovered, island that was once called Christendom. For it did truly appear, as in a dream, that the island had grown large; and that I had landed on something larger than a continent. For Christendom is much larger than Europe. Even in the Middle Ages it was much larger than Europe. I am not arguing here about the claims of various sorts of Christians to inherit the full tradition of Christendom. I only say that to see even so much of Christendom in one place was like seeing a vision; like being taken to the top of a mountain and seeing all the kingdoms of the earth. If any bright wit from Portadown or Belfast retorts that the Devil, in the person of the Papal Legate, would naturally take me there, I am content to bow and smile.

The historical point to realise is that this last grey island, lying out in the homeless Atlantic was at that moment crowded like Cosmopolis and a kind of capital of the world. It was not the normal and delightful, experience of visiting Dublin. Indeed I found it physically impossible to visit many of the friends whom I most enjoy visiting. Yet faces, familiar and unfamiliar, in the crowd, somehow produced the same impression of a sort of sociable nightmare. It was not the same place; it was not perhaps any place. It was more like a dream of the Day of Judgment.

I will take only one or two of the vivid figures walking in that waking dream. Thus, I have been for months in America; but I never saw a real American Indian in America. But I saw one in Dublin. He walked about in the streets with his tremendous tiara of plumes towering up like a grove of palm trees. Under that was the unmistakable high-featured face moulded in copper; the red relentless mask of our boyhood's dreams. And under that was the dark decorous vesture of an ecclesiastic; for this man was both a Red Indian chief and a Roman Catholic priest. The most detached type of traveller will agree that one would not see that figure walking down the street every day. Or again; I have been to Palestine; and I saw many Greek priests in Palestine. But I have never seen a man dressed as a Greek priest when he was actually a Roman priest. But the distinguished representative of the Roman obedience, who had come all the way from Russia, looked exactly like any Orthodox priest of the old Byzantine Church of Muscovy; wearing the strange Rabbinical head-dress and the imposing beard, which gives a nameless touch as of something Assyrian, something primeval and patriarchal, to the stiff and stately patriarchs; as if the great Basilica were supported by winged bulls instead of cherubim. Yet this man was an ordinary Papist like any other; like myself or the nearest gutter-boy in Dublin.

Another strange figure, and unfamiliar name, raises the point still more pointedly. Suppose an ordinary Englishman, or for that matter an ordinary Irishman, were told that there was a Jacobite priest in Dublin. His mind would instantly go back to Patrick Sarsfield and the wars of Derry and Limerick, in the days when the Catholic Irish were Jacobites. He would think the

Jacobite priest was perhaps a little too much concerned with the past; but it is a complaint often made about the Irish. And since the Northern Irish continue to remember the Boyne, there seems no reason why the Southern Irish should not continue to remember the Stuarts. And then he would suddenly discover that a Jacobite does not mean a Jacobite[1]. It means something enormously older, infinitely remote, something apparently quite alien from the other side of the world. It concerns the re-conversion to Catholicism of an ancient Asiatic heresy, which wandered away and lost itself somewhere at the beginning of the Dark Ages; probably following the forgotten mysticism of the Monophysites. The dignified Indian gentleman who represented this far-off triumph in the Orient, had changed his neighbours by bringing them back into the Roman Communion; but he had changed in nothing else. By the look of him, he might have walked that moment out of any Hindoo temple covered with bulbous imagery, or any Persian mosque scrawled with a fantastic script. He wore a sort of tall turban for a mitre; his keen and vigilant face looked browner and darker behind his grey luxuriant beard; his vestments were of a cut and pattern new to all the Western world. At the first careless glance, he might have been anything; the private chaplain of Genghis Khan or the High Priest of the cult of the Holy Monkey or the Sacred Snake. For we in Europe

[1] Jacobites are members of the Christian church tradition of the Middle East founded by Jacob Baradaeus in Syria, who were considered heretical by Rome. However after contacts were renewed in the 17th Century, some entered into Communion with Rome, and one of these was present in Dublin. The Jacobites in the British Isles were the adherents of James II and his heirs, the Catholic claimants to the throne of Great Britain and Ireland, the last of whom was a cardinal in the Catholic church. Ed. note.

are generally very vague about distinguishing one Asiatic dress or dignity from another. Only, in his hand he carried something that was not the sign of the snake or the ape, or any wild cult of the sort that had perhaps surrounded it for centuries ; it was that strange sign that was once the shape of the Roman gibbet and still represented to him the divine paradox of Rome.

For the moment I merely sketch these strange figures as strangers; in order to suggest the almost unearthly strangeness of the scene. For I believe about the Eucharistic Congress, as I believe about the universal cosmos, or for that matter about every weed or pebble in the cosmos; that men will never rightly realise that it is beautiful, until they realise that it is strange. Pantheism has been attributed to the poets; but in truth Pantheism is the very opposite of poetry. Poetry is that separation of the soul from some object, whereby we can regard it with wonder; whereas Pantheism turns all things into one thing, which cannot wonder at itself. And the first feature to note in the spiritual drama of Dublin was this spirit of strangeness. The eccentric figures from the ends of the earth were only emblems of this wonder of the world; but they were emblems of it. Something of that allowable margin of myth and magic geography, that can be found in the popular legends of Christendom, painted these that came from the East and the West to sit down in the Kingdom with strange colours of the sunrise and the sunset; with the mythologies of the sun and moon and the four corners of the world. I began to feel quite creepy about the man with the turban and the cross; remembering that he was from the talismanic land of India and looked like a Rajah, and yet had the chrism of a Christian priest. I wondered if it was Prester John after all[2]. At that point Prester John disturbed my dream, by suddenly coming up to me and saying in excellent English that he had read some article of mine in a newspaper. I soon discovered that his conversion of the Jacobites had been a highly intellectual and even modern process; a part of a quite lively contemporary controversy now going on all over the world. And, in spite of his reading the newspapers, nay even my articles in the newspapers, he was exceedingly well read. I felt a certain vague confusion, and I still feel that I never thanked this distinguished prelate adequately for his remarkable courtesy and kindness; but there is something disproportionate in finding one's own trivial trade, or tricks of the trade, amid the far-reaching revelations of such a trysting-place of all the tribes of men. But it is typical of the intellectual unity of that religious world, that this strange priest from the land of sunrise instantly tackled me about all sorts of immediate and important questions; and was so magnanimous as to ask me to be photographed with him on the steps of the Vice-Regal Lodge.

I could imagine no reason for his selection; unless it were that we were, in very different ways, the most curious objects in that landscape; I had a vague idea that I might be acting as a sort of mascot; as if he were being photographed with the sacred White Elephant for a background[3]. But as I bowed myself away from his only too gracious conversation, I admit I had another disturbing thought. I remembered that in Asia the presence of a half-wit or lunatic is regarded as lucky, or a protection against the evil powers. And, though I cannot suppose a Catholic bishop, especially so intellectual a bishop, to be subject to superstitions, the doubt did recur to me afterwards, from time to time.

Beginning with these distant outposts, which stood up most clearly against the remote horizons, the imagination began to work inwards, through the infinite labyrinth of Christendom. I had the honour of meeting a German bishop, who ministered to the Germans in Danzig; his intellectual interests were German; his immediate ancestry was German; and his name was O'Rourke[4]. He was the descendant of one of those wandering soldiers, called the Wild Geese, who went forth from a defeated Ireland to win victories for alien princes all over Europe; and in his case, I suppose, as far north as Prussia. A minute or two afterwards I was introduced to the hierarchs of the great Catholic civilisation of Poland; and I knew I had crossed an abyss which

---

[3] White elephants were awarded by the Kings of Siam and other Indochinese states as a way of imposing a wearisome burn on the overambitious. They had come to prominence in the 1880s with the arrival of one in England in January 1884, and the term became popular slang for any unwanted object one was anxious to be rid of. Ed. note.

[4] By the treaty settlements after WWI, a corridor of land was provided to Poland to give the state access to the Baltic port of Danzig, thus cutting off Eastern Prussia from Germany proper. This became a bone of contention between the two states and was eventually the *casus belli* of WWII. Ed. note.

has, at least, no other possible bridge but that made by the bridge and builder: the Pontifex Maximus[5]. Just after that I was talking to a priest from Lithuania, with whom I made a desperate attempt to converse in Latin; under all the disadvantages of having learnt it for six years at an English Public School.

So one might easily move, in centripetal curves, to the very core of Europe. There was nothing and nobody concerned in the great Continental controversies, who had not some sort of representatives there. Only all these men who disagreed in politics agreed in religion. It was impossible not to fancy that some sort of political agreement might best begin here, where there was at least an agreement upon something.

But, however this may be anybody of any belief or unbelief must have had the same sensation in the same scene. He must have felt, even before he felt that he was in the beautiful city of Dublin, that he was in the practical centre of Europe. He must have felt that ring behind ring, of those concentric circles of Europe, were closing in upon a centre. Dublin was Lausanne: and Lausanne with a common speech, unlike Babel[6].

One of the foreign bishops who made himself particularly popular in Dublin was the Cardinal Archbishop of Paris: a remarkable man in more ways than one. For one thing, by I know not what intelligent instinct, he went straight for the strangest

---

[5] An imperial Roman title, adopted in later Christian times by the Popes, meaning "great bridge builder". Ed. note.

[6] The Lausanne Conference was a 1932 meeting in Switzerland, held from June 16 to July 9, 1932, of representatives from Great Britain, Germany and France that resulted in an agreement to suspend World War I reparations payments imposed on the defeated countries by the Treaty of Versailles. Ed. note.

and most refreshing revelations of the place; and explored all the popular festivity and decoration in the poorest quarters. So far as I know, he had never been in the slums of Dublin in his life. But he understood them with an inspired intelligence which met the true test of the time.

He bought up all the medals or badges of the Congress, and went down to distribute them among the poor like bread. Probably nobody will believe me when I say that the poor were better pleased than if he had distributed sixpences. But until that incredible truth is understood, all this incredible story will have been told in vain.

When I realised such sincere and even simple touches of true international sympathy, when I remark on the fact that even anti-clericals would hardly deny that most priests are well-meaning, and trained in some minimum of altruism and self-control, and when I look at the senseless, selfish anarchy around us, my mind goes back to that vague suggestion which I made about Danzig and the diplomatists. I have no notion how it could be done, under modern limitations; but I strongly suspect that, as in earlier times, priests would make very good diplomatists. For they alone have already an international law to which to appeal. I do not mean that they are bound to agree. On the contrary, I mean that they alone are free to dispute. For a dispute must begin somewhere; and most modern disputes not only end no-where, but also begin nowhere. I may mention again that case of the threat of Prussia to Poland, which, I am quite certain is the threat of War to Europe. It is not a matter on which I pretend to be indifferent, which is what most people mean by impartial. I have always had strong opinions on Poland as on Ireland. I will confess that I even find it difficult to understand any Catholic not sympathising with Poland against Prussia; especially now that Prussia once more means Prussianism[7]. But at least the German Catholic cannot support Prussianism, even if he sup-ports Prussia. I personally think it is mere nonsense to call a vast expanse of ancient Polish territory a corridor, merely be-cause a much more artificial little *enclave* called East Prussia has been stuck in the middle of it like a pin. So far as I can see, in all sincerity, it can only mean one of two things. One is that Prussia would like to repeat the Partition of Poland; or in other words, that Prussians are so stupid that they still cannot believe that the Poles exist. The other is more miserably comic still. For it means that the Prussians truly repent of what the Russians did; and will make full restitution of what the Austrians stole; and will only keep what they stole themselves. I state my views thus strongly, precisely because I wish to insist that I could state them strongly to a German Catholic, who accepts my stand-

[7] The allusion is not to the Nazis, but to the German military rearming under the Weimar Republic. Adolf Hitler, the leader of the National Socialist Workers Party, was not elected Chancellor until January 30, 1933. The Third Reich only came into existence in August 1934. Ed. note.

ards, but should hardly think it worth while to state them to a Prussian materialist or atheist, who does not really accept any standards. The very fact that I have instinctively put my point about the Partition in terms of the Catholic doctrine of repentance and restitution exactly illustrates the understanding that I mean. The German Catholic might answer me; but he would have to answer in the same language, and answer the same question. However German he may be, however pro-German he may be, he cannot, for instance, describe his proposed Partition in the form of a breezy jest against the Blessed Sacrament, as did that enlightened eighteenth-century philosopher whom Germany remembers as Frederick the Great, who invited the other sovereigns, as to a supper-party, "To partake of the Eucharistic Body of Poland."

The tired and tiresome voice of the general secularism talks with eternal reiteration about the quarrels of theologians. One would suppose that nobody had ever quarrelled except theologians; or that theologians had never done anything else. But if there be one thing morally certain, it is that the world will quarrel much more without theology than it ever did with theology. In logic, this is self-evident; for people left without any common theory, or attempt at a theory, will be able to quarrel about absolutely anything whatever; including all the things on which men have hitherto agreed. For instance, those who disagree in theology must at least agree in theism. But if a man is free to be an atheist, he is free to be a polytheist; and if he is free to be a polytheist, he is free to set any god against any other god; he is free to start an entirely new god and set him against all the rest; say a god with nine noses and fifty fingers, or any other product of evolution and the advance from the simple to the complex. I need not say that the last figure is a figure of speech; for I willingly admit that modern thinkers have not enough imagination to make a mythology. But they can make as much confusion in their metaphysics as any savages could make in their mythology. They can take up ultimate positions, which all theologians of the past, or indeed all thinkers of the past, would have called anarchical and abnormal; but from which they cannot be dislodged, simply because they are ultimate positions. They are out of sight and hearing, for the purpose of anything so sociable as a quarrel. Men do not agree enough to disagree. Thus, for example, there is no sense in reasoning with a man who denies any validity in reason; it is vain to convict of injustice a man who declares his disbelief in justice; it is idle to offer ocular demonstration to the really consistent sceptic, who cannot believe his eyes. There have always been individuals of this sort; but the trouble is that, since the religious schism, whole nations and cultures have come to take up collective attitudes more or less out of touch with humanity and normality; Prussianism and Bolshevism, and even Fascism; for Fascism without Catholicism might easily have hardened into something utterly inhuman. Once remove the old arena of the theological quarrels, and you will throw open the whole world to the most horrible, the most hopeless, the most endless, the most truly interminable quarrels; the untheological quarrels.

A German priest may have something to say against Poland; a Polish priest most certainly has something to say against Germany. And as each has something to say, it is possible that on proper occasion he may say something. But he will not say anything, in the sense of everything and nothing; the one will not say anything that comes into his head against Germany nor the other against Poland. The German priest will not say, "We are going to make war on Poland, for, as our great German sage has said, a good war justifies any cause." The Polish priest will not say, "Nationalism is more important than Catholicism; and if I can exalt the Polish nation, I don't care if all German Catholics go to hell." The Polish priest and the German priest, as such, cannot deny the dogma of justice, of the lawful loyalty to one's own nation, of the duty of extending mercy even to another nation, and so on. But the Pole and the German, as such, can deny anything whatever. Once suppose both of them to be freethinkers, and there is nothing to prevent one defending tyranny as such and the other anarchy as such. There was a time, I know, when these crazy negations were supposed to be peculiar to cranks; it is even possible that they are still largely peculiar to cranks. But what is emphatically not impossible is for the cranks to become the rulers of the commonwealths. The commonwealths are drifting away from each other in ideas; as Prussia drifted away from Europe before the War; as Russia drifted away from Europe after the War. How far the heresy is actually held by anybody but the heresiarchs, might well be a matter of dispute; though it looks as if the heresiarchs did make a good many heretics. The point is that, before they drift too far apart, while some of them are within hailing distance, some use might be made of a central group which contains men of all countries, men generally very loyal to their countries, but men having also the quite unique advantage of a common code of law and justice, and the protection of a sort of permanent courtesy, more deeply founded than the fiction of diplomacy, which is called the profession of Christian charity, and forbids them, at least beyond a certain point, to despise or insult or wantonly exasperate each other. If it concerned any other group except the Catholic Church, anybody would see that what I say is common sense.

My meaning will be quite mistaken, if anybody supposes I want a Fifth, Sixth or Seventh International, or anything that is commonly meant by Internationalism. An International Council commonly fails, because it consists of picking internationalists out of all the nations. But that is just the point. Priests are not internationalists; they are only normal nationalists, or, at any rate, normal nationals. An Irish priest and an English priest are not in the least likely to be people who have forgotten their nationality. They are only people who are not allowed to forget their humanity. But all those whose theories are merely human soon forget their humanity. It was theorists and not theologians who forbade patriotism, as the Prohibitionists forbade beer. It was the poets and not the priests who howled that any butchery or barbarous enslavement was allowable in the fury of patriotism, as the drunkards demand any amount of beer. In both cases the Church will generally be found, not merely more moderate, but emphatically more liberal, than the extremists who alternately dominate the merely worldly councils of the world. It is idle to answer, what is obviously true enough, that men may hold a moderate or liberal theory and yet betray it. The question is whether any other men will long have any theory to betray.

By the beginning of the Middle Ages, that is by the time that the Dark Ages showed they were capable of giving birth to a new civilisation, priests are found everywhere in the position of statesmen and diplomatists and leading government officials. This was not because other men were not ambitious, for many men were much more ambitious; it was simply because other men were not competent. It was found in practice that a Scottish chieftain merely broke down in negotiations with a Scandinavian sea-king, because, though both were brave and enterprising and very probably shrewd in their own affairs, they simply did not possess enough general knowledge to fit themselves into other people's affairs. The world had broken up into little states, just as it has now broken up into little sects. Since then, we have seen the final phase of dissolution; when even the sect breaks up into little philosophers; generally very little philosophers. Each one is living in a cosmos of his own, and it is more difficult than ever to establish any agreement between the separate sages, who have broken from the separate sects, who have broken from the original body of our culture. It seems to me that the future will need quite as much skilled intervention, between individual intellectuals, as ever the past did between divided groups. If psychology and philosophy go on dividing and subdividing, everybody will be talking a different language; and will need a *lingua commums*, even more than did the Middle Ages. It will be necessary to have an interpreter between a Behaviorist and a Fundamentalist, as much as it ever was to have one between a Breton and a Frank. And in the original case, the Interpreter was an Interpreter, because Latin was a larger language; the large utterance of the older gods.

It is rather a joke that enlightened moderns should boast of being Anti-Clericals, when we consider the real meaning of Clericalism. In practice the Cleric only meant the Clerk and the Clerk only meant the man who could read and write. That Henry the First was called Beauclerc did not mean that he was known everywhere as The Beautiful Clergyman; it meant that he was what we should call an educated man. But it was true then, and it is becoming more and more true now, that to be anti-clerical is really to be anti-cultural, or anti-educational. For unless there can be created some sort of international interpreters, with an international grammar and code, it is appallingly true that there is nothing before us but Babel; and a confusion not merely of tongues. All our immediate ancestors did to avoid it was to divide the multitude more strictly according to the tongues; to summon them all to a Council armed to the teeth; and to kill the Interpreter.

III

VERY CHRISTIAN DEMOCRACY

LENIN said that religion is the opium of the people. This profound remark will readily explain the sleepy submission, the supine placidity, the dull and drowsy obedience of the Irish people; as compared with the wild revolutionary frenzy, the incessant insurrection and revolt, the bloody riots and endless street-battles of the English people. Nobody who has been in Dublin for a week as I have been during the Eucharistic Congress, can doubt that Ireland is passionately religious; and especially that the Irish populace is passionately religious. It therefore follows, by the strict logic of Lenin, that the Irish populace has always been particularly patient and subservient and contented. Nobody who has lived in England all his life, as I have, can doubt that modern England, with its many manly and generous virtues, has become largely indifferent to religion. It follows therefore, by the strict logic of Lenin, that the English are the best Bolshevists in the world. To suppose anything else would be to indulge in the audacity, nay the blasphemy, of supposing that there is something wrong in the logic of Lenin. We must therefore believe, as best we can, that the Irishman has always been a tame and timid person; and that it is the Englishman who has always been "agin' the Government." The inference is that it is only by believing in God that we could possibly believe in the Government. But the truth is that it is only by believing in God that we can ever criticise the Government. Once abolish the God, and the Government becomes the God. That fact is written all across human history; but it is written most plainly across that recent history of Russia; which was created by Lenin. There the Government is the God, and all the more the God, because it proclaims aloud in accents of thunder, like every other God worth worshipping, the one essential commandment: "Thou shalt have no other gods but Me."

Lenin only fell into a slight error; he only got it the wrong way round. The truth is that Irreligion is the opium of the people. Wherever the people do not believe in something beyond the world, they will worship the world. But, above all, they will worship the strongest thing in the world. And, by the very nature of the Bolshevist and many other modern systems, as well as by the practical working of almost any system, the State will be the strongest thing in the world. The whole tendency of men is to treat the solitary State as the solitary standard. That men may protest against law, it is necessary that they should believe in justice; that they may believe in a justice beyond law, it is necessary that they should believe in a justice beyond the land of living men. You can impose the rule of the Bolshevist as you can impose the rule of the Bourbons; but it is equally an imposition. You can even make its subjects contented, as opium would make them contented. But if you are to have anything like divine discontent, then it must really be divine. Anything that really comes from below must really come from above.

*   *   *   *   *

The gossip which I wrote a few pages back, about some of the guests of the Congress, was largely filled with the figures of certain foreign prelates or patriarchs, in whose externals there was something that seemed almost fantastic, and even outlandish, to anyone who does not realise how far the most adventurous of all religions has penetrated to the outer lands.

And I think that even this mood has a certain value, as telescoping the two ends of Catholic truth; the remoteness of its scope and the nearness of its daily habit. In fact I fancy that Catholics take a certain almost ironic pleasure in the strangeness, or even the stiffness, of certain ancient forms or Oriental emblems; precisely because they know that in the core of them is a Christian simplicity and charity, and that they can only frighten those who do not know what they mean. The more we are proud that the Bethlehem story is plain enough to be understood by the shepherds, and almost by the sheep, the more do we let ourselves go, in dark and gorgeous imaginative frescoes or pageants about the mystery and majesty of the Three Magian Kings. It has even some affinity with a sort of joke; by which we should find an intimate message from a friend slowly spelt out from old Egyptian hieroglyphics or Babylonian cuneiform. And certainly this, or one aspect of this, was the first impression produced by the immensely imaginative panorama of the first Benediction services in the Phoenix Park.

In the centre, over the altar, arose the dome of a sort of temple, picked out in dark tawny red and a not too glaring gold; and on either side were two great pavilions for the Cardinals, dyed of a rather duller red than their robes. Something in the two shades, as of two kinds of red lacquer, something also in the angular pattern of the criss-cross lines above them, gave the whole a curiously Chinese appearance; so that even the faces of Englishmen and Irishmen, whom I know perfectly well, took on an almost spectral remoteness, not merely of place but of time; as if they were indeed long-withered Mandarins looking out of vermilion pavilions under the First Dynasties of the Sons of Heaven. Outside these again, there swept out in two long horns the terraced seats of the Bishops and Archbishops. And this in turn produced another historic illusion; for the whole crescent was a sort of colonnade in which hung baskets of green plants, that might have been the laurels or the olives of the Mediterranean; and the Bishops sitting under them in their purple robes looked like Roman Senators looking down upon an amphitheatre. And in both cases the imagination could play freely with the irony; remembering that none of these sublime incongruities could ever be incongruous; that the Church did in truth set up her first house in Pagan Rome; and may yet set up her hundred temples in Pekin.

I have said I quite understand an honest outsider being a little puzzled by this pontifical pomp; which seems somehow to be at once worldly and yet unearthly.

But though the eye was first and most naturally attracted to the external and even extraordinary signs and symbols of that colossal hierarchy, there was something else also, which was even larger and not less mysterious. The relations between the two things could not be better conveyed than in the incident which happened to connect them, in my own case.

A Bishop, towering above me in all the terrors of that imperial Roman purple, stepped down suddenly and asked me, with a very broad brogue, to go a step or two above him and look out over the whole Park. I did so, and looked around me, and saw far out to the very edges of the sky that immense spiritual sea that is called The People.

It was very like a vision; at least I fancy I saw several things in that vision which I shall find it very difficult to describe here or anywhere else; so I will begin with one of the least of them.

*   *   *   *   *

The Eucharistic Congress concerned the Eucharist; and the word Eucharist is but a verbal symbol, we might say a vague verbal mask, for something so tremendous that the assertion and the denial of it have alike seemed a blasphemy; a blasphemy that has shaken the world with the earthquake of two thousand years.

But when once we have realised that everything was concentrated on this, with a simplification unknown in most modern life, certain secondary truths appear, and they are very curious and interesting. They should be rather specially interesting to those who do not share the dogma that was the centre of interest. The very fact that the vast multitude of men was looking only at that central altar will give the outsider an opportunity of looking at them. If he does, he will realise certain facts (which they would regard as being on a lower plane of politics or social science), but which he will find curiously apt and topical.

To take but one instance; I confess I was myself enough of an outsider to feel flash through my mind, as the illimitable multitude began to melt away towards the gates and the roads and bridges, the instantaneous thought: "This is Democracy; and everybody is saying there is no such thing."

I do not mean it in any merely sentimental, or even merely sympathetic sense. I do not mean anything about brotherhood or fellowship or social idealism. I mean it in the definite defiant sense of the actual Greek word; I mean the crowd ruling itself, like a king.

If there is one thing about which the modern mind is utterly sceptical, it is this. It is far more sceptical about this than about any ancient miracle, even the miracle of the Mass. It is nonsense to say that no scientific modern minds now believe in the Mass. But it is very nearly true to say that no scientific modern minds now believe in the Mob. If we take all the current statements about the gradual decay of all dogmas of Christianity, we shall find that they are pretty roughly true, if we apply them to the dogmas of Democracy. The commonest form of denial, especially among the most cultivated and capable critics, is the denial of that dogma of Rousseau, which is called "the General Will." The Humanists of America, the Fascists of Italy, even the Bolshevists of Russia, all the most recent schools that have revolutionised the old revolutionary tradition, all dismiss this democratic mystery as a myth. There is no such thing as a General Will. How could there be a General Will?

Now it is quite certain that a General Will walked about the streets of Dublin for a week. It is quite certain that there was practical harmony, because there was theoretical unity. There was truly and actually, in the threadbare and vulgarised phrase of the politicians, a Will of the People; and it did prevail. The order was not only organisation. It is true that the organisation was very good. Anybody who shall say henceforth that the Irish cannot organise, or cannot rule, or are not practical enough for practical politics, will certainly have the laugh against him for ever. There has never been a modern mass meeting, of anything like this size, that passed off so smoothly, or with so few miscalculations or misfortunes. But nobody who looked at the crowd could for one instant mistake its order for organisation. The mob could be managed successfully, because every man in the mob passionately wished the ceremony to be a success. They were men of many minds on many other matters, including politics, but on this they were of one mind; that is, they had a General Will. That mob, alone among modern societies, had self-government. It really had self-government, in the old sense of self-control. If it had not been organised, it would have organised itself. It was a vision very extraordinary, to any man who has seen the bewildering facts of modern politics, and compared them with the monotonous repetition of modern abstractions. It was the Self-Determination of the People.

As it happened, there was a simple test or comparison. There had recently been a General Election in Ireland, ending in a majority and minority of the usual Parliamentary sort. It elected Mr. de Valera as President; and that in the regular recognised way of electing a President. But no man in his five wits would have supposed that such a crowd would combine for Mr. de Valera; or that any chance member of it was necessarily a supporter of Mr. de Valera. If one had pointed suddenly to any particular person, some seedy little tradesman or lumbering clodhopper from the country, no man would risk a shilling on the bet, "That man voted for de Valera." He might be a supporter of Mr. Cosgrave, who received rousing ovations everywhere; he might be a stubborn survival of the old Nationalists; he might be an old Catholic Moderate who had actually been a Unionist; he might be a happy fellow who had never heard of politics at all;

he might be anything. That is the real point about Democracy; and Rousseau was really right exactly where his critics say he was wrong. There *can* be a General Will; but it is not the same as an electioneering, majority; and nobody in the first democratic days ever thought it was. It may be a convenience to govern by clockwork majorities; but it is not what the real Republican meant by the Will of the People.

So far, the moral seems to be rather strange; that this great political ideal can exist; but cannot exist in politics. Certainly it seems rather the reverse of the ordinary present practice of politics; which is devoted rather to seeing how men can be most equally divided, than how they can be most fundamentally united.

Whatever may be said in practice for a Party System, it is obvious that the idea of the Party System is almost the exact opposite of the idea of the General Will. But that is another question, which I need not debate here, though I may perhaps recur to it in another connection. The point for the moment is that the only thing in modern times, that can really produce anything resembling this old ideal of the politicians and political theorists is Religion. Nothing else could really unite as all those people were really united; not a successful revolution, not a decisive election, nor any other sort of practical experience found on the earth today. What I saw spread out before me was in a very exact sense of the word Christian Democracy; not as the label of a party, but as the living achievement of a people. A whole mob, what many would call a whole rabble, was doing exactly what it wanted; and what it wanted was to be Christian. And I sometimes wondered whether even political democracy would not be a little more practical if people prepared for the General Election as they did for the Eucharistic Congress, with prayer and penance rather than with publicity and lies.

In truth, without tracing such speculations too wildly, I may say that the incident left me with a strong suspicion that nobody will ever discover the moral truth there is in modern democracy, until it is really conducted in a Catholic atmosphere. I mean, of course, an atmosphere that has not been corrupted at all by the gas and hot air of a modern commercialism. I fear it would be fantastic to expect Catholic democracy to be conducted on the lines of the heroic virtues. It would be too much to hope that every candidate would begin with a complete confession of his crimes, instead of a catalogue of his virtues. It were vain, perhaps, to hope that the really best men of the village, the truly chosen of the people, would be dragged desperately struggling out of their houses and forced to be reluctant Members of Parliament, as St. Anselm was forced to be a reluctant Archbishop of Canterbury. But I have a strong notion that a real reversal of the present routine in such things might prevent political power being, as it is now, a direct reward of self-advertisement. For I fancy there is a deep truth in democracy which democrats have never discovered. It could only be discovered by seeking for those who think themselves least worthy to rule, or even least worthy to vote. However this may be, it is certain that every revolution in human history has failed solely because it could only fulfil half of the revolutionary maxim of the Magnificat; it was true again and again, and often very justly, to cry aloud: *Deposuit potentes de sede*; but no revolution has ever yet achieved the sequel: *Exaltavit humiles*.

Yet, since this is the only point at which I even touch on politics, I will add a word to avoid a misunderstanding. The Congress was accompanied by two portents, remarkable by their rarity. One was that in the Atlantic Islands (my sensitive impartiality will not permit me to call them the British Islands) there was actually summer weather in summer. The other was that, broadly speaking, for a whole week, there were no politics in Dublin. This does not mean, of course, that men's political attitudes or feelings altered; that would be a poor compliment either to them or their politics. But it does mean that, barring a small blunder or two, the public mind was concentrated not on politics but on religion. I should not like anyone to think, how-ever, that I underrated the politics, or put them second to any-thing except the religion. I should be sorry if my remarks about the difference between a General Election and a General Will were taken as partisan, or involving any pronouncement on the present Irish problem. I happen to have a very great respect for the new President of the Irish Free State, as one of the very few men who have at least realised that the whole modern capitalist cosmopolitan civilisation is already in collapse; and that it *may* be a wise operation, though it is obviously a dangerous opera-tion, to cut a country completely out of that web or network and make it separate and self-supporting. On the other hand, I was so placed in a social sense as to be able to bear testimony to the loyalty, the dignity and (I will add) the generosity with which the official representative of the existing connection maintained the honour of his office, without doing a shadow of wrong to the honour of his opponent. I think it right to say that amid all the Irish intensity there was a very fine clarity of intellectual jus-tice; and I have heard the same man on the same night propose the health of the King, in conditions that made it as dramatic as a bomb at a Conservative club, and afterwards defend the char-acter of Mr. de Valera with a spirit and emphasis as memorable as any accusation. I think this much due to the much-abused bitterness of Irish politics; and I must add, somewhat mournfully, that even when they are bitter they are clear. For I know very well that, fond as I am of the geniality and humour of my own countrymen, when I returned to England, to a country where people read the newspapers, I found myself back in a fog.

IV

THE PHOENIX IN THE PHOENIX PARK

WHEN I returned after Mass, on that last amazing Sunday in the Phoenix Park, to the house that had so nobly entertained me, I walked about for hours in long avenues or large quiet rooms, worrying and trying to resolve a certain problem. It was the highly practical problem of how, or whether, it was possible to convey to the world at large what an astounding thing had just happened in the Phoenix Park; a sensational event much more truly sensational, and properly much more of an event than the Phoenix Park Murders. I was not specially thinking of writing it then, as I am writing it now, for Catholic readers. Catholics know that the Mass is the Mass and in a sense can never be more magnificent than the Mass; but they would understand every attribute that made the magnificence more apparent. But though we walk the world as three hundred millions, I sometimes feel that we are still in the Catacombs; we still talk by signs like the Cross and the Fish, or at least with a secret language. And I sought in vain a language that would tell ordinary outsiders of something not in the same world with their normal notions of a sect or even a service; something which must either be expressed in the august theology they have forgotten, or in some sort of epic poetry which nobody now can write. The only thing I could think of was the parallel with the whole Pagan tradition and its witness to the world's need, not of worship, but of sacrifice. It was under the weight of these peculations that I wrote down the words that follow.

*　　*　　*　　*　　*

I cannot trace the name of the Phoenix Park, but it is quite certain that it contained a Phoenix. If I were simply to say, in the old straightforward style of the storytellers that we assembled to see the burning of a gigantic golden bird, as big as an ore and as beautiful as a hundred peacocks, who was consumed to ashes before our eyes; after which the golden feathers sprouted again out of the golden flames, and that vast and radiant monster rose again and ascended visibly into heaven – if I were thus to fulfil my duties as a conscientious reporter, there would be some so mean and small-minded as to complain of errors of detail in the report.

But it would be a very much more vivid and solid statement

of what actually did happen, than if I merely stated that a Eucharistic Congress was held in Dublin and attended Mass in the large park round the Vice-Regal Lodge. The very nature of the neighbourhood was a reminder that something quite extraordinary had been completely burnt out and had somehow survived its own burning, and that on the very place where a strange spiritual monstrosity was destroyed because it was incredible, it had proved itself undeniable by proving itself indestructible. For the bird called the Phoenix was the ancient symbol of resurrection, as the bird called the pelican was the symbol of charity. It was merely a trivial accident that the Phoenix never existed and the pelican never was particularly charitable to anybody; so much the worse for the pelican.

*   *   *   *   *

But the figure of the Phoenix will serve as a symbolic introduction; because it has been used more than once by Irish poets even of the more Pagan school. Mr. W. B. Yeats recently wrote very touchingly of one of those beautiful women of Ireland who have done so much for her liberty, and been the muses of her poetry; and threw a tolerant encouragement to younger men innocently contented with younger women; saying: "I knew a Phoe-

nix in my youth; so let them have their day." Even in reading
that spirited poem, I was struck with a certain inconsequence
in the image. For the Phoenix of legend is not merely a dog who
has his day. He is a bird who very much outstrips the cat in the
possession of nine lives. But the pagan poet, by the very nature
of paganism, called the dead lady a Phoenix, in the sense that
she was as unique and marvellous as a Phoenix; not in the sense
that she was as immortal as a Phoenix; certainly not in the sense
that she would instantly rise from her ashes like a Phoenix. It is
not a lack of sympathy, but rather a sign of sympathy, with Mr.
Yeats' intensely imaginative and individual magic and power, to
say that all such praises from him have a burden of finality, if
not futility; and he does really regard love as "a perpetual fare-
well." The extraordinary thing we have to deal with here is a
belief as defiant as the most literal fable; a bird that can be burnt
to ashes and continue to fly. For those who disbelieve in it, even
more than for those who believe in it, it is an astounding historical fact that a poem can be acted before millions, as a fact and not
a fiction: by which is truly killed and made alive, not one woman
who lives in the memory of one man, but one Man who has lived
in the memories of men since He died in the most distant days
and regions of the Roman Empire. This is that part in poetry
which is played by memory, multiplied on so colossal a scale that

even a pagan may well admit that it is something of a portent in the midst of modern society.

In other words, that which blazed on that strange altar under that strong summer sky was indeed a Phoenix, in his sense as well as ours. It is altogether inadequate to call it a religion. It is in some ways more nearly true to call it a myth, which is also a fact. It has nothing to do with shades of opinion or shifting theories of mere philosophy. It is nearer to what is symbolised in those solid and splendid and most objective objects, for which giants and gods and heroes strove in the mythological morning of the earth. It satisfies the need for actuality and appeasement of which that shining solidity was a symbol; the golden ram of Colchis or the golden apples of the Hesperides. It was not a theory; nor even merely a thought; nor anything to be spoken in any human word. It was an Achievement. It was an Act. It was therefore in the true sense epic; where even the best of modern religion is only lyric; and a good deal of it elegiac.

I was stationed very near the domed and gilded shrine I have already described; at the corner of one of the vast encampments which cut up the whole huge plain into squares; like the assemblages of the tribes in some tremendous primitive revelation. I could hear directly almost all that was directly addressed to the congregation, which was carried everywhere elsewhere through the resounding mirrors of the loud speakers. But I think every-one who heard all those things, directly or indirectly, will agree *salva fide* and apart from the invariable values of the Canon, that the most astonishing thing they heard was something that they could hardly hear. At one of the moments when Catholics would be accustomed to hear the clear and rather shrill tinkle of the bell of the Sanctus, there was heard a sound that must be almost unique in human history. It was as faint as the sound of a far-off sheep-bell and as weak as the bleat of a sheep; but there was something in it that was not only weighty, but curi-ously hard; almost dead; without the resonance that we mean by music. It was as if it came out of the Stone Age; when even musical instruments might be made of stone. It was the Bell of St. Patrick; which had been silent for 1,500 years.

I know no poetical parallel to the effect of that little noise in that huge presence. Some such imaginative nerve was once touched for me, in a context quite incongruous and infinitely less important, by one fine artistic instinct in Rostand's play about the only son of Napoleon. That play is simply filled with the name of Napoleon; and the author was far too clever to sug-gest the ghost of Napoleon, or even the ghost of a ghost of Napo-leon. But an old Napoleonic soldier dies in delirium, dreaming of the last charge at Wagram and the victory. And among the last noises of battle, the rush of horse-hooves and the rest, there is heard, tiny and clear and infinitely far away, just the voice beginning: "*Officiers; sous-officiers; soldats* . . ." and then no more. That is as near as the ghost comes to his ghost story. Multiply that by a millionfold more of import and intensity than all the greatness of Napoleon; extend that by twelve times the length of time that separates us from Napoleon; and it was something like that little distant voice, that was heard for a moment by all those thousands. From far away in the most forgotten of the centuries, as if down avenues that were colonnades of corpses, one dead man had spoken and was dumb. It was Patrick; and he only said: "My Master is here."

And after that, I for one could realise little but a catastrophic silence, till it could be crowned with the only fitting close. From the four corners of the sacred enclosure the all-shattering trumpets shouted, like the Sons of God shouting for joy. And all along the front there ran, like a sudden lightning, the light upon the lifted swords; for all the soldiers standing before the altar saluted with a blazing salute of steel, carrying the hilt to the head in the old swordsman's salutation, and then striking outwards, in the ancient gesture of the Romans.

Her face was like a King's Command when all the swords are drawn.

The old line of Belloc's song went through my mind for a moment; and none could doubt in that day what King was commanding; almost visible upon His throne. There are those who tell us we must broaden our ideas, by which they mean disembody or discolour them, in order to make a universal religion for men; and that particular rites or forms or holy places will shut us out from our fellow-creatures of all climes and colours; and that these therefore must be replaced by abstractions. The truth is flatly the other way. It is by these particular signals and symbolic gestures that the race of men as a whole does, and always did, recognise a religion. If all the Pagans who ever worshipped strange gods had strayed into Ethical Societies or Unitarian Chapels, their very first word would be: "But where is your altar?" And so in that tremendous instant of the volleying trumpets and the fan swords, the ages dropped from us and even the distances of all the many-coloured earth; and we knew that we *should* be understood by everything human, and especially all that has remained most human. For if there had been looking down, from the hills round Dublin, the wild heathen chiefs who first looked down when that primeval bell was tolled, or if the ships in the bay had been the ships of Scandinavian sea-kings watching from afar, or if all who could be conscious of that lonely dome standing up under the steepness of the sky had been

Pagans from the ends of the earth, they would have known in that noise and light, and by a flash of universal understanding, that the God had descended among men.

How that instantaneous but intense conviction, that those bases of humanity which are most human, even when they are heathen, can still understand the thrill which the Greeks called enthusiasm or the god dwelling with us – how that can be properly conveyed through the jaded jargon and cheap Cockney culture, that is far more of a mask for man than any mere ignorance or superstition, I am still unable to resolve. But I rather think that somebody will have to write a religious poem.

Let no man answer that I am preaching a conversion by beautiful catastrophe; by theatrical thunder and parade of arms. Anyone suggesting this will suggest the very opposite of all I say, or have ever said. No man could be received into the Catholic Church if he were converted by a clang of trumpets or an old Celtic bell. I myself should utterly distrust my own conversion, if it had only taken place at the moment of supreme exaltation in Phoenix Park. A man who finds his way to Catholicism, out of the tangle of modern culture and, complexity, must think harder than he has ever thought in his life. He must often deal as grimly with dry abstractions as if he were reading mathematics with the hope of being Senior Wrangler. He must often face the dull and repulsive aspects of duty, as if he were facing the dreariest drudgery in the world. He must realise all the sides upon which the religion may seem sordid or humdrum or humiliating or harsh. He must feel all the counter-attractions of Paganism at least enough to know how attractive are those attractions. But, above all, he must think; above all, he must preserve his intellectual independence; above all, he must use his reason. It would be better to reject the Faith than to accept it as an unreasonable thing. I do not say, and I have never said, that the splendour and wonder of these things can be the same as the final satisfaction in them. I say that all real human religions would recognise the reality of this as a religion; but that is not the same as recognising it as *the* religion. I may say that even the heathen, when they are human, would realise the presence of Christ, their foe and their friend; but it would not always answer the old question: "Your gods and my gods; do you or I know which is the stronger?" I do not say that the man who merely feels these things is by that act accepting this thing. To do that he must reason more closely than any rationalist; yes, and think more freely than any freethinker. He must broaden his mind much more than any of the broadminded; it is the compliment of the ancient truth: "Unless your righteousness exceed the righteousness of the Scribes and Pharisees." Unless your inwardness and sincerity exceed that of all the intellectuals who talk about inwardness and sincerity, I do not say that even the miracle of the Phoenix will convince you. But I do say this.

I say that *when* you are convinced, when you are rationally convinced, when you have come to the end of the long road of reason, when you have seen and seen through the tangled arguments of the time, when you have found the answer to them – *then* you will find yourself suddenly in the morning of the world. Then you will find yourself among facts and not arguments, but facts as marvellous as fables; facts like those which the pagans pictured as a land of giants or an age of heroes; you will have returned to the age of the Epic; and the epoch of things achieved.

V

THE MISSION OF IRELAND

As the Congress week drew to its end, the patch of glowing weather which had been stretched like a golden canopy, strangely and almost insecurely, began to show signs of strain or schism. There was a hint of storm in the still heat, and here and there random splashes of rain. It was naturally a topic of anxious talk, and it gave birth to one great saying, which I shall always remember as one of those tremendous oracles that sometimes come from the innocent. A priest told me that he had heard a very poor threadbare working woman saying in a tram, with a resignation perhaps slightly touched with tartness: "Well, if it rains now, He'll have brought it on Himself."

This remark fitted with a queer exactitude into certain vague reflections of my own. They took the form of telling myself that I was at least entitled to pray that it might not end in a drizzle. If we could not have the strong sunshine, the next best thing would be that it should all end in one stark, startling, shouting, shattering thunderstorm; like the thunderstorm that is said to have

accompanied the deliberations of the Council on Papal Infalli-
bility. Our enemies would doubtless say that thunderbolts were
being hurled at our impious idolatry; but it would be more dignified than merely being damp. But when I heard the dark saying
of the woman in the tram, I suddenly realised that the storm
above the shrine would really express a duality which is one of
the paradoxes of the Faith. For that great truth uttered in the
tram is one of those truths that are all the more true, because
they seem to mean half-a-dozen different things at once. They
can be taken in various and even opposite ways; as can so many
examples of French irony, polished and deceptively simple. The
woman's remark might be taken as a simple and even touchingly literal expression of faith; it might be taken as a Voltairean
sneer; it might be taken again, as I suggest, as one of the most
profound and inscrutable of the double truths of Christian theology. For indeed, if the sky grew black above the canopy of gold,
or the great monstrance blazed in the storm-flash instead of in
the sun, or the temple was hung with dark curtains of tropic rain
and the trumpets drowned in the thunder, it would be but the
symbolic staging of a contradiction in the core of the Christian
mystery; the God without seeming to sacrifice the God within;
the very world of the Creator turned against the unworldliness
of the Crucified; the Father accepting the death of the Son. The

remark of the woman in the Dublin tram, among other things, was a remark that might very well have been made by Caiaphas or Pilate. He has rather a way of bringing it on Himself.

As has already been implied, the fears were groundless, and the good weather held up to the last and supreme day of Celebration. But the reflections I have made on the reported remark and the potential thunderstorms, continued to run much in my mind, until I thought I began to see yet another aspect of the mystical truth of the tram. I will leave it to the theologians to define and even to rationalise in so far as mysteries can be rationalised; but using in my ignorance a merely popular and picturesque language (like the prophetess in the tram), I may be permitted to suggest in a general way that there is this double aspect in everything Christian, a double aspect that corresponds to the Dual Nature of Christ. There is a spiritual specialism in both aspects; sometimes it is needful to stress one and sometimes the other; but there rose in my thoughts a shadowy historical theory; at the end of which I saw in some sense transfigured, and like a truth made new, the greatness and the significance of Ireland.

We talk of the Faith turning the world upside down. There is a deep and rather indescribable sense, in which it turns the world inside out. Among the wild abstractions of mathematics there is an idea which cannot present itself to the imagination in any image, however monstrous; which is a purely logical necessity. It is a process by which the sphere is turned inside out, the centre becoming the circumference and the circumference the centre. Something like that is among the paradoxes of Christianity, which are so puzzling to those True Christians who can only understand the platitudes of Christianity. Christianity was like that impossible mathematical figure. Christianity was a whirlwind which was the inversion of a whirlpool. There was in the heart of it some mysterious centrifugal force by which the heart passed outwards to the extreme limit of the limbs. It was not always safe to look for the centre in the centre; certainly not to look for the life in the root. This paradox is suggested in many dark sayings in the New Testament; about the lightning shining from the east unto the west, or the children of the kingdom being cast out. They seem to suggest a remote ring of light running like a halo round the horizon; even in the day when all is darkest at the centre; and the Abomination of Desolation is sitting in the Holy of Holies.

This mystery is a fact even of history and geography. In any case, it is plain that even the home of Christ was only the place where He was homeless. It is also true in a more strange fashion of the whole secular history and destiny of that devoted place. The scene of the Incarnation seems to have become almost sealed and consecrated to the denial of the Incarnation. Before the coming of Christ, it was ruled by those Jews whose high monotheism eventually hardened and narrowed into a violent refusal of the Incarnation. After the coming of Christ it was ruled by those Moslems, who also interpreted monotheism mainly as the denial of the Incarnation; even after the Incarnation. But even between the Mosaic and Moslem systems, which emphasised a disembodied divinity before and after Christ, there was a multitude of mystical developments, tending in the same direction and thriving especially in the same neighbourhood. We too often forget that the Monophysite who came before the Moslem had fundamentally much the same mood as the Moslem. Heresies thronged through all the cities of the Near East, through all the roads trodden by the Apostles, all loudly denying the doctrine of the double nature of Christ; which was the essential paradox of the Incarnation.

Most people know that the Monophysites were the very opposite of the Modernists. Whereas the most recent heretics are humanitarians, and would simplify the God-man by saying He was only Man, the most ancient heretics simplified Him by saying He was only God. But these mystics had in their hearts the same horror as the Moslems: the horror of God abasing Himself by becoming human. They were, so to speak, the anti-humanitarians. They were willing to believe that a god had somehow shown himself to the world like a ghost; but not that he had been made out of the mere mud of the world like a man. And the odd thing is that these cries of horror, at the very possibility of such a blasphemy happening, were most wild and shrill round the very place where it had happened.

It would be inhuman not to pity the poor Modernist or Humanitarian or Higher Critic, who set out so confidently to find the real origins of Christianity in the original country of Christ. He naturally felt that the nearer he came to the stones of Jerusalem or the grass of Galilee, the more simple the story would appear; that in the place where Jesus had lived a human life, He would admittedly appear most human; that among the actual natural surroundings would be found the most natural explanation. If the critic had been approaching any of the common kings or heroes of history, it probably would have been true; that to find them in their homes would be to find them when they had laid aside the crown and sword, and the terrible postures of history. As the critic was approaching the perplexing Carpenter of Nazareth, it was not in the least true. There was no purely human tradition of any purely human Jesus. In so far as there was any tradition at all, lingering in the fights and factions of Greek and Judaic religion, it was the tradition of a purely divine Jesus.

It was a tradition furiously upheld by all those traditionalists who wished to represent Him as wholly and solely divine. Only the orthodoxy of the Catholic and Apostolic Church declared that He was in the least human. And above all, for this is the point of the paradox, the Catholic Church proclaimed that original humanity more and more loudly, as it passed away from its original human habitation. As the Church marched westward she bore with her, with ever-increasing exultation and certitude, the human corporeal thing that had been made flesh in Bethlehem; and left behind a ghost for the Gnostics and a god like a gilded idol for the Greek heretics, and for the Moslems only the fading shadow of a prophet.

It may be repeated that the emphasis on this truth, if not the truth itself, actually grew stronger as the Church marched westward, from Antioch to Rome and from Rome to the ends of the earth. And there is really a certain confirmation of this view; in the fact that the mere expression of the truth, apart from the truth itself, gathered new forms of power and beauty, as its long travels took it not only far from Jerusalem, but even far from Rome. The ends of the earth shall praise Him; and some of them had powers and methods of praise that were not known even to the more civilised centre. It is true that this was only a matter of clothing the Incarnation in garments; as the Incarnation was itself a matter of clothing the incredible in flesh. But it is interesting to note that the original human nature, which the Modernists seek in its oriental birthplace, and the Monophysites most indignantly denied in the neighbourhood of that birthplace, unfolds itself in physical imagery most fully in the extreme occidental outposts that recognise the leadership of Rome. The Higher Critics took a frigid pleasure in referring to their human Christ only as Jesus of Nazareth; but they could not find Him in Nazareth. They could find little or nothing in Nazareth or twenty other holy places of the East, but the flattened faces of the Greek icons or the faceless ornament of the Moslem script. In so far as He was remembered, or at least in so far as He was imagined, as a human personality and a Man moving among men, He was seen moving as in a hundred pictures, under Italian skies or against Flemish landscapes, a new Incarnation in colour and clay and pigments; which did not take place till He had reached the coloured regions of the sunset. This contrast is true, to some extent, even where the eastern tradition is orthodox and not merely "Orthodox." The tendency was always to make the image a sort of diagram of divinity; even when it was not the dark inhuman diagram of the Monophysites and the Manichees. Even the true theologians were *theologians*; they defended rather than described the Humanity. Western Christendom, the new empire made entirely by Rome, discovered this Humanistic development. It made the first portraits, if not the first pictures of Christ.

In one aspect Protestantism may well seem a bigger and sillier blunder than any involved in its original doctrines, or its present absence of doctrines. It might be put very shortly and crudely by saying that the Reformation attacked the Roman Church for the faults of the Greek Church. It might be expressed, in a mere rough symbol, by saying it did not realise that Rome was itself rather in the West than in the East. Anyhow, it assumed that Catholicism was merely stiff with gold and stark with dogma, complex in ornament, tied to a ritual remote from life; depending on mere antiquity, a gilded mausoleum; a whited sepulchre. But whether this was true or false, it was much truer of that Oriental Christianity, schismatic or even heretical, than it was of the Roman Christianity that had escaped from it by going West. If it had gone East, it would only have sunk further and further into a deep but glowing night of transcendentalism, like a tropical forest in its luxuriance and in its inhumanity; full of the faceless images and bewildering diagrams of divinity without humanity; the Asiatic religions of the abyss. There are even some dark and fearful Christs, in the more sinister phases of Byzantine art, which really look Monophysite to the point of monstrosity;

and we almost look to see a wheel of six arms, holding hammers and thunderbolts. Meanwhile, the purely human figure of the Carpenter, carved by carpenters or craftsmen as simple as carpenters, was already rising on shrines and pedestals far away, in the crypts of Rome or the niches of Rouen. There was something symbolic, like a mysterious repetition of the Flight into Egypt, in the way in which the Mother, carrying the Divine Humanity in her arms, took refuge in the Roman world of the West; and seemed still to be fulfilling some destiny even in moving continually westward. It was as if, in some fairytale about sunset and the islands of the blest, there was to be discovered somewhere a softer air or a more quiet light, in which the God could most freely show Himself as a Man; taking on an intimate and domestic character forgotten in the heat and the hard abstract feuds of the fiery places of His birth. Western art, Western legends, Western customs of Christmas or Easter, gradually unfolded the fulness of the Manhood, with which dwelt the fulness of the Godhead bodily. It was not, of course, what modern sentimentalists mean by a human Christ; for that is not a human Christ, even if it is a human Jesus. But it is something that is, up to a point, perhaps better expressed by craftsmen and carol singers than by controversialists and merely combative dogmatists; and to develop this domestic, poetic and popular sentiment, in the complex of Catholicism, has been even for early times the mission and function of the West.

Ireland, combining a remote position with a close loyalty to the Papacy, was enabled to be, if we may use both words in their rarest and best sense, at once Roman and Romantic. Her religion has always been poetic, popular and, above all, domestic. Nobody who knows anything of her population will think there was ever any special danger that her Deity would be only a definition. He was always so intimate as rather to resemble, in a pagan parallel, a household god or a family ghost. Ireland was filled with the specially human spirit of Christianity, especially in the sense of the pathetic, the sensitive and the great moral emotions that attach to memory. But Ireland had to develop this element under conditions that differentiated her from most Catholic countries. She was too poor and too oppressed to shelter the Divine Humanity under the roof of mighty cathedrals or even to paint His coloured shadow upon frescoes or palace walls. Lying so far north, she had been caught in a bleak intellectual blizzard that was as dry and destructive as the sand-winds of the Iconoclasts and the Manichees. She went down in a struggle with the northern heresies; especially with a Calvinism that came rather from the Scotch than the English, but which was unfortunately supported by the whole force of English wealth and war material. Under these circumstances her natural western mission of asserting the Divine Humanity was not only checked and limited, but even when it grew stronger, took on a particular character.

The praise of embodied divinity took on the disembodied character of words or even of silence; of a speech that had the intensity of a whisper; of a tradition that was compelled to all the vigilance of a conspiracy. But the whole was so vividly of this positive and personal sort, that I have little doubt that the return of liberty and prosperity to Ireland will mean the development of that Christian craftsmanship, in which she once taught the world in the decorative designs of the Dark Ages. Any impression so atmospheric must appear arbitrary, and it would be idle to mention the multitude of small experiences that have seemed to me to point to such a destiny. I will only mention two things out of a thousand; one an old story which I heard and even recorded long ago; the other a small incident that quite recently happened to myself; but in both of which is expressed with a certain emotional exactitude the shade of fact and feeling that I mean. The first is a story I heard in Donegal twelve years ago; but I know nothing of the origin of the story. It told how someone had met in the rocky wastes a beautiful peasant woman carrying a child, who, on being asked for her name answered simply: "I am the Mother of God, and this is Himself, and He is the boy you will all be wanting at the last." I had never forgotten this phrase, which expresses the spirit of which I speak in a language which is a natural literature; and I remembered it suddenly long afterwards, when I fancied I had found something that expressed it also, not in literature but in sculpture.

I was looking about for an image of Our Lady which I wished to give to the new church in our neighbourhood, and I was shown a variety of very beautiful and often costly examples in one of the most famous and fashionable Catholic shops in London. It was a very good shop, and the proprietor was not to blame if the nature of the find was something of a parable. It is the glory of the great cult of Mary that she has appeared to painters and sculptors under a variety of bodily types almost wider than the actual variety of all the women in the world. She has been the patroness of so many lands and cities that she has become the centre or the prop of every scheme of ornament or school of architecture; and her garments have been made of all the materials of the world. Here there was everything, from what some would call the conventional dolls of the Repository to what some would call the harshest caricatures of the Primitives. But somehow I felt fastidious, for the first time in my life; and felt that the one kind was too conventional to be sincere and the other too primitive to be popular. There were types of the bronze Byzantine gloom and types of the cereal Flemish exuberance ; extravagances of Renaissance drapery, wrought in enamel or in metal, sprawling like a wheel of wings yet poised like a pillar; delicate figures in ivory or dark figures in ebony; all the multiform manifestations of the most profound inspiration of the arts of our race. But, for some reason, as I have said, they left me not indeed cold but vague, and I ended prosaically by following the proprietor to an upper floor, on some matter of mere business; the receipting of an old bill or what not.

But the upper room was a sort of lumber room, full of packages and things partially unpacked, and it seemed suddenly that she was standing there, amid planks and shavings and sawdust, as she stood in the carpenter's shop in Nazareth. I said something, and the proprietor answered rather casually: "Oh, that's only just been unpacked; I've hardly looked at it. It's from Ireland!"

The colours were traditional; but the colours were not conventional; a wave of green sea had passed through the blue and a shadow of brown earth through the crimson, as in the work of the ancient colourists. The conception was common and more than common, and yet never merely uncommon. She was a peasant and she was a queen, and in that sense she was a lady; but not the sort of sham lady who pretends to be a peasant, nor the sort of sham peasant who pretends to be a lady. She was barefoot like any colleen on the hills; yet there was nothing merely local about her simplicity. I have never known who was the artist and I doubt if anybody knows; I only know that it is Irish, and I almost think that I should have known without being told. I have heard of one other man who felt as I do, and went miles out of his way at intervals to revisit the little church where the image stands. She looks across the church with an intense earnestness in which there is something of endless youth; and I have sometimes started, as if I had actually heard the words spoken across that emptiness: *I am the Mother of God, and this is Himself, and He is the boy you will all be wanting at the last.*

Finis